Captured in Miniature
Mughal Lives through Mughal Art

Suhag Shirodkar

Mapin Publishing

This edition published in 2010 by
Mapin Publishing Pvt. Ltd
502 Paritosh, Near Darpana Academy
Usmanpura Riverside
Ahmedabad 380013 INDIA
T: 91 79 402 28 228 | F: 91 79 402 28 201
E: mapin@mapinpub.com | www.mapinpub.com

Simultaneously published in the
United States of America by
Grantha Corporation
77 Daniele Drive, Hidden Meadows
Ocean Township, NJ 07712
E: mapin@mapinpub.com

Text © Suhag Shirodkar
Illustrations © as listed

All rights reserved under international copyright conventions.
No part of this book may be reproduced or transmitted in any form
or by any means, electronic or mechanical, including photocopy,
recording or any other information storage and retrieval system,
without prior permission in writing from the publisher.

ISBN: 978-81-88204-83-0 (Mapin)
ISBN: 978-0-944142-61-5 (Grantha)
LCCN: 2010923269

First published in India in 2007 by
Mapin Publishing
in association with
HarperCollins *Children's* Books, an imprint of
HarperCollins *Publishers* India

Typeset in Adobe Garamond Pro
Designed by Lorena Zalles and Janki Sutaria / Mapin Design Studio
Edited by Diana Romany / Mapin Editorial

Printed and bound at Thomson Press, India

Not for sale in the Indian sub-continent

List of Illustrations

The Mughal Dynasty

Page 7: *Portrait of Babur*
Musee Guimet, Paris

Page 8 (below): *The Marriage of Humayun and Hamida*
Cynthia Hazen Polsky Collection, New York

Page 11: *Akbar Hands his Crown to Shah Jehan* (Minto Album)
Chester Beatty Library, Dublin

Royal Lives

Page 15: *Akbar Supervises the Building of Fatehpur Sikri*
Victoria and Albert Museum, London

Page 19: *A Prince and Holy Men in a Garden*
Chester Beatty Library, Dublin

A Love for Nature

Page 23: *Squirrels in a Plane Tree*
British Library, London

Page 26–27: *A Zebra*
Victoria and Albert Museum, London

Dress and Costume

Page 31: *The Sehra Ceremony of Prince Aurangzeb*
Royal Library, Windsor Castle

Page 34: *Portrait of Nur Jehan*
Raza Library, Rampur

Celebrations

Page 37: *The Birth of a Prince*
Boston Museum of Fine Arts

Page 41: *Jehangir Playing Holi*
Chester Beatty Library, Dublin

Royal Pursuits

Page 44–45: *Akbar Stages a Shikar near Lahore*
Victoria and Albert Museum, London

A Painter's Life

Page 49: *Artists at Work*
Prince Sadruddin Aga Khan Collection

Page 53: *Daulat the Painter and Abd al-Rahim the Scribe*
British Museum, London

For
Dr. Anand J. Bariya
and
Dr. Milo C. Beach
—both provided inspiration, but only the former could temper it with spousal skepticism

For
Mohini and **Mallika**
—at 10, delightful writers already

And

For
The San José Public Libraries
—which make so many endeavours possible

Contents

Introduction		6
The Mughal Dynasty		7
Royal Lives		14
A Love for Nature		22
Dress and Costume		30
Celebrations		36
Royal Pursuits		44
A Painter's Life		48
Resources		56

Introduction

Almost 600 years ago, an ambitious Central Asian prince swept down from his mountainous homeland and conquered Delhi, a fabulously rich city in northern India. The prince was Zahir-ud-din Muhammad Babur. Babur's descendants, called the Mughals, established a mighty empire that dominated India for two centuries. With their passion for nature and art, the Mughal emperors laid out verdant gardens, built splendid monuments (including the Taj Mahal) and commissioned beautiful books.

Books were precious to the Mughal kings. Expensive and laborious to produce, they were symbols of royal wealth, power and intelligence. At the height of Mughal power, the imperial studios hummed with the activity of hundreds of papermakers, calligraphers, painters and bookbinders, all producing books for the royal libraries. Many manuscripts were illustrated with exquisite miniature paintings, in which the Mughals took a special delight. Today these books and paintings, treasured by museums around the world, offer us unique perspectives into Mughal lives.

Mughal miniatures were usually painted on paper, and occasionally on cloth. A typical miniature was only as large as this page. Within such limited space, artists painted spectacular battle and court scenes, or elaborate nature studies. They painstakingly created life-like portraits no more than an inch high. They captured the tassel on a courtier's belt, or a glass of wine cupped in a royal hand. Such minute work required delicate brushes made from a few pliant hairs of a squirrel's tail.

Mughal emperors took great pride in their artists' work. They frequently told them what to paint, reviewed their drawings, and rewarded them handsomely for producing a particularly fine piece of art. Because of this close association between artist and patron, Mughal miniatures reveal much about the kings themselves—of their lives, their interests, and what they wished to be remembered for. Of the hundreds of Mughal paintings still in existence, we could reproduce only a handful in this book. Nevertheless, we hope they will provide a glimpse into the colourful, and endlessly fascinating, Mughal Empire.

The Mughal Dynasty

Babur, the first Mughal king, loved gardens. When the artist Payag painted this portrait, many years after Babur's death, he created a setting that would have delighted the king. Babur is portrayed seated on a carpet set upon a grassy mound. A stream bubbles gently over mossy rocks. Fragrant flowers surround Babur, as he gazes upon the jewel in his hand.

A gilded book rests on Babur's lap. The book may represent his famous memoir, the *Baburnama* (The Story of Babur). Throughout his years in Delhi, Babur missed his home in Central Asia, and his feelings shine clearly through in the *Babur-nama*. He writes about his longing for the snow-capped peaks, the broad-leafed trees, and the juicy melons of Ferghana. He complains about hot, dusty Delhi although he enjoys its monsoon rains. The nicest thing about India, writes Babur, is that it is 'a large country with lots of gold and money'.

Here are portraits of the great Mughal kings and the years in which they reigned.

Babur 1526–1530

Babur, like all the Mughal kings after him, believed that his dynasty had the support of god and heaven. Look carefully at the borders around the portrait to see how the artist depicted this belief. A pair of angels keeps watch over the haloed king. To the right, three priests hold copies of the Koran, the holy book of Islam. Below the portrait, a yak, a timid herd animal, stands fearlessly close to a lion. Babur ruled with such justice and wisdom, implies the artist, that animals even lost their fear of predators.

Humayun 1530–1539 and 1555–1556

In 1530, after Babur's death, his son Humayun became king. Defeated in battle by an Afghan chieftain, Humayun fled west to Persia. There he took shelter at the court of his cousin, Shah Tahmasp. When he returned to India several years later, he brought home two of the Shah's most accomplished painters, Mir Sayyid Ali and Abd us-Samad. Although Humayun did not realize it, his bringing back the Persian painters established the course for Mughal art in the centuries to follow.

In spite of his efforts, poor Humayun could not commission many fine paintings in India. A few months after regaining the throne of Delhi, as he hastened to his prayers, he tripped on the stairs of his library and tumbled to his death. The Persian painters, however, continued to work in the studios of Humayun's son, Emperor Akbar.

Akbar 1556–1605

Akbar, a dynamic and energetic king, rapidly expanded the royal studios. Soon, hundreds of artists were working in his studios, guided by the Persian painters and by the king himself. A vigorous Mughal style of painting quickly evolved as an intermingling of Persian direction and Indian tradition.

Jehangir 1605–1628

Shah Jehan 1628–1658

Jehangir and Shah Jehan both took great interest in painting. During their reigns, artists became more specialized. Some artists painted only animal studies, while others only portraits. Yet others became expert at painting official court scenes. The kings closely directed and delighted in the work of their artists.

Aurangzeb 1658–1707

During Aurangzeb's rule, the Mughal Empire, and Mughal art with it, began to decline. Later kings became progressively weaker and lost most of their wealth as well as large areas of their territory. Finally, in 1858, Bahadur Shah II, the last Mughal emperor, was defeated by the British colonizers and exiled to Burma.

Akbar Hands His Crown to Shah Jehan

In 1631, Bichitr, whose name means 'wonderful', painted this miniature of the three greatest Mughal emperors. At the centre, on a golden throne supported by angels, sits Akbar. To the left of the picture is his son Jehangir. To the right, receiving a jewelled crown, is his grandson Shah Jehan. The king's ministers stand attentively in front of them. Although all six portraits are realistic, this is not a real situation.

The painting depicts Akbar handing his crown, symbol of the Mughal dynasty, directly to his grandson. Jehangir, watching silently, appears displeased at being thus ignored in the line of succession.

To appreciate this painting fully, you must understand the relationship between Akbar and his son. During Akbar's reign, Jehangir rebelled and battled against his father. He established his own court in the city of Allahabad and proclaimed himself king. He even plotted to have his father's best friend murdered. Although father and son patched up their differences when Akbar grew old, the tension remained. Bichitr portrays this deep-rooted conflict by showing Akbar bypassing Jehangir and handing the crown directly to his grandson. This picture was painted during Shah Jehan's reign. Would Bichitr have dared paint it while Jehangir was alive?

The Mughals enjoyed compositions like this, in which symbols are used to tell a story. We call them allegorical paintings.

Mughal painting flourished under these three kings. Unfortunately, Aurangzeb, the last of the great Mughals, was a very conservative Muslim. Believing that painting living beings was against Islam, he took no interest in painting and began withdrawing support from the royal artists. During his reign, Mughal art went into a decline from which it never recovered.

Royal Lives

Akbar Supervises the Building of Fatehpur Sikri

It was 1568 and Akbar had been emperor for over 20 years. Under his able and wise leadership, the Mughal Empire was enjoying stability and prosperity. Still, the emperor was a worried man. Mughal custom dictated that only a male child could inherit the throne. And Akbar, though he had several wives, had no son.

15

The emperor decided to seek the advice of a holy man named Shaikh Salim Chisti who lived in Sikri, a small town many days' journey from Agra. Shaikh Salim predicted that a prince would soon be born. When that prediction came true, a joyous Akbar decided to honour the Shaikh by moving the Mughal capital from Agra to Sikri.

A brand new city had to be constructed in Sikri. Forts, palaces, bazaars and stables had to be built. Emperor Akbar took personal interest in the proceedings. In this bustling miniature, we find him inspecting the construction of his new palace. Shielded from the sun and fanned by attendants, the white-robed emperor talks to a stone carver while an attentive clerk takes notes.

This miniature brings alive the toil that went into constructing Akbar's palace. At bottom left, a bearded trader and his youthful helper lead in two bullocks loaded with sacks of lime. Lime, or calcium oxide, was used to make mortar during the Mughal times. Two women squat in the midday heat. One sieves the lime, while her companion pounds and crushes brick with a stone mallet. Close by, an old man mixes the crushed brick and lime to make the mortar that he shovels into a labourer's basket. Up the wooden gangplank march the muscular labourers, baskets securely atop their heads, delivering bricks and mortar to the bricklayers.

The palace at Sikri was made of bricks and sandstone, a red sedimentary rock excavated from the surrounding hills. Hundreds of sandstone carvers from Rajasthan were employed at Sikri. Here we see them driving wedges into slabs of sandstone to split them along their length. A completed sandstone screen is visible behind the carver whom Emperor Akbar is addressing.

Did you notice that we appear to be watching this busy scene from high above? The artist is using what is called perspective, or point of view. Use of perspective allowed Mughal artists to fit complexity and detail into a small area. The gangplank, running diagonally, also accomplishes this same objective. Exquisite details lend an additional spark to this painting.

How many tiny birds can you spot in the painting?

A Prince and Holy Men in a Garden

In contrast to the bustle of building Fatehpur Sikri is this picture of calm and relaxation. The talented Bichitr painted Prince Dara, Jehangir's pensive son, meeting in his garden with a group of holy men. They are probably discussing philosophy and religion, subjects dear to Dara's heart.

How cleverly Bichitr captured the solemn, intense mood of the evening! Two holy men engage the prince in discussion. One rests his hand upon a Koran while his neighbour leans forward, eager to catch the prince's words. The greybeard to the left appears lost in deepest thought. To the right, two musicians sing to the accompaniment of a *tanpura*, a stringed folk instrument fashioned out of a hollowed gourd.

Kneeling before a little table, an attendant pours wine. Notice how meticulously Bichitr painted the flasks, the fluted glasses and the stack of white porcelain cups on the table. Even a tiny stopper for the wine carafe has not been forgotten.

Did you spot the three attendants in the background?

One of them is preparing Dara's bed for him. Are the other two discussing some accounts or bills, perhaps?

Look at the courtier clutching his shield, at the bottom left of the painting. He's staring out of the picture, and straight at you. Why do you think the artist painted him like that?

Was he trying to portray the courtier as detached from, or bored of, the philosophical discussions taking place? Or was the artist trying to create a connection between his painting and his viewer—*you*?

A Love for Nature

Squirrels in a Plane Tree

Emperor Jehangir, like the Mughals before him, enjoyed nature. When a flower, bird or animal caught his fancy, he quickly ordered his artists to make a painting of it. Inspired by Jehangir's boundless curiosity and his almost scientific interest in exotic creatures, some of his artists mastered the art of painting birds and animals in their natural settings. A lovely example is this miniature, called *Squirrels in a Plane Tree*.

On a sunlit autumn day, bright-eyed squirrels gambol in a tall chinar, or plane tree. They arch their tails, ready to spring from branch to branch. Two hungry babies peer eagerly out of their nest, waiting to be fed by their watchful parent. Pairs of birds nestle in the chinar's sturdy branches. It is a happy scene.

But why is a barefoot man attempting to scale the tree? Is he a hunter on the lookout for squirrel meat? Is he an artist collecting squirrel hair to make paintbrushes? Can you feel the tension that his presence creates in the painting?

Scholars think that many artists worked together to paint this miniature. They think Abu'l Hasan painted the tree and Mansur the squirrels, with junior artists filling in the background. Such cooperation, once common in Mughal studios, became increasingly rare during Jehangir's reign.

A Zebra

Emperor Jehangir enjoyed strange animals so much that he had his own zoo. Knowing this, visitors to the Mughal Court brought him strange creatures from distant lands. One morning, as Jehangir was meeting with his courtiers, an excited murmur rose through the halls. A bizarrely-striped horse, brought in by a visitor from Abyssinia (modern-day Ethiopia), was being led towards the imperial throne.

Jehangir and his courtiers were astonished. Never before had they seen such a creature. Why, they wondered, would anybody paint black stripes on a horse?

Stepping down from his throne, the emperor inspected the strange arrival. After several minutes of scrutiny, he declared that the stripes on the creature were the work of the divine creator, and had not been painted on by human hand. Then he immediately ordered Mansur, one of his favourite artists, to make a painting of the animal.

The keenly observant Mansur created this delicate painting of the exotic creature. He expertly captured the softness of its gaze, the gentle arch of its back and the strength of its haunches. So accurately did he depict it that we easily recognize it as a Burchell's zebra, native to the plains of Africa and commonly seen in zoos around the world.

29

Dress and Costume

The Sehra Ceremony of Prince Aurangzeb

Appearance and dress were very important at the Mughal Court. Clothing was not only functional and beautiful, but symbolic as well. A nobleman's clothes and accessories indicated his rank, his religion, and how favoured he was by the emperor. European visitors write of being dazzled by the splendid jewels and silken robes they saw at the Mughal Court. Of course, special occasions, such as a royal wedding or the emperor's birthday, demanded even richer clothing and adornment.

Here is a painting of a ceremony that took place on the night of May 18th, 1637. Prince Aurangzeb, seen bowing before his father Shah Jehan, is to be married at daybreak. In keeping with Mughal custom, the emperor prepares to tie a *sehra* around his son's forehead. The *sehra*, a shimmering veil of pearls and precious stones, concealed a Mughal bridegroom's face during his wedding ceremony.

Bending low before the emperor, the youthful Aurangzeb seems weighed down by his finery. He wears a gold-spun jacket over a flowing silken robe and tight pleated trousers called *achkan*. A jewelled sword is tucked into his brocade cummerbund. Rubies and emeralds adorn his turban. Lustrous pearls glow at his neck, arms and wrists. Aurangzeb smiles gently, as if he knows what a handsome picture he makes.

Emperor Shah Jehan is splendidly dressed as well. Notice his golden robes, his gem-encrusted belt and dagger, and the rings on his fingers. Around him stand princes and noblemen, all dressed for this happy occasion. But a close look through the latticed balcony reveals only unshod feet. It appears the Mughals had adopted the Hindu custom of taking off their footwear as a mark of respect for authority.

Today, Indian men rarely wear traditional clothes like those shown here. Many Indian women, though, continue to dress like the women in this painting.

A large company of musicians performs below the balcony. They sing traditional wedding songs to the accompaniment of drums, tambourines and fervent clapping. The women wear short blouses and long skirts, exposing their midriffs. Veils and jewels drape around their necks. Some women have dyed their fingers with henna to mark this special occasion.

Portrait of Nur Jehan

Mughal women observed purdah, which means that they lived in secluded women's chambers and could not be seen by any man other than the king. For this reason, there are very few paintings depicting Mughal women or their lives. Nur Jehan, Jehangir's strong-willed wife, opposed such strict seclusion and encouraged more freedom for women.

Here is a rare and powerful portrait of Nur Jehan, painted by Abu'l Hasan. Ready for a hunt, Nur Jehan, an excellent marksman and shooter, is dressed in classic Mughal hunting gear. The flowing robe, tight trousers and turban that she wears here were usually worn only by men. A bag of ammunition is tied at her waist.

Jehangir delighted in Nur Jehan's hunting skills. In his memoir he writes how she once shot four tigers from atop an elephant, killing each with a single shot. So pleasing was this performance, says Jehangir, that, 'I presented her with diamond bracelets and showered her with gold.'

Celebrations

The Birth of a Prince

Here is a rare view into the zenana, the secluded palaces for royal women. The occasion is momentous. Akbar's Rajput wife, Maryam al-Zamani, has just given birth to a baby boy who will grow up to become the Emperor Jehangir. While the queen rests in the birthing room with a gentle smile on her lips, a midwife prepares to place the swaddled prince in a golden cradle. Akbar's mother, seated on a throne just outside the room, is quietly delighted at the birth of her grandson.

How revealing are the expressions of the women gathered around!

Although some appear pleased, others look unhappy, annoyed or envious. The zenana was typically a hotbed of gossip, suspicion and intrigue. Women competed with each other to win the favour of the emperor. Having produced an heir, Maryam would receive special attention from Emperor Akbar, so many other women would be upset.

For this happy occasion, the arched entrance to the zenana has been decorated with garlands. A curtain drawn across the archway prevents visitors from peering in. But it does not stop a curious maid from peeking out at the trays of sweets and gifts being carried to the zenana doors.

On a carpet outside the fortifications sits a trio of astrologers. With charts and divining tools, they draw up a horoscope for the royal baby, predicting his future and the power and glory he will attain. Shortly, the emperor will have the horoscope read to him.

Do you think the astrologers would predict anything other than a glorious future for the royal baby?

Jehangir Playing Holi

Holi, the festival of spring, was celebrated in Mughal times almost exactly as it is today. Revellers used metal water guns to squirt each other with coloured water. They showered brightly coloured powders on each other, a metaphor for the flowers of spring.

In this picture, two ladies of the zenana lead Emperor Jehangir to the Holi festivities. In the carpeted courtyard of the zenana, women—their hands and feet dyed with henna—sing and dance. One woman appears to have gotten some of the red powder into her eyes; another forces bhang (an intoxicating drink much enjoyed by the Mughals) down her comrade's throat.

Notice how richly the zenana is decorated. Patterned carpets cover the floor, and murals decorate the walls. The mural of the pair of deer appears in several Mughal miniatures and may likely have been a real painting on the zenana wall.

A cat sits silently on a porch, watching the revelry from a safe distance.

What is the mood of this picture? Do the women look as if they are enjoying themselves? Does this painting give you a sense of life in the zenana?

Royal Pursuits

*Akbar Stages
a Shikar near Lahore*

Agra, the Mughal capital, was surrounded by dense jungle teeming with cheetah, fox, boar, deer and other wildlife. Mughal emperors sallied forth into these jungles to enjoy their favourite sport—hunting. Their hunts were massive, complex and bloody operations that required weeks of planning.

Several days before a hunt, thousands of footmen, or beaters, marched into the forest to form a vast human circle many miles in diameter. Blowing horns or beating on drums, they flushed animals out of the thickets. Every day they moved slowly forward and inward, so that the creatures were corralled into an ever-shrinking circle.

At night, they lit torches around the periphery of each camp to prevent animals from escaping in the darkness. When the circle became sufficiently small, they built a stout fence of posts and netting. Thousands of animals were trapped inside the fence, easy targets for the imperial hunt.

In this chaotic two-panelled painting, the young Emperor Akbar appears engrossed in the pleasures of the hunt. First with bow and arrow and next with sword, he pursues the panicked creatures that make futile bids to escape. Captive collared cheetahs assist with the hunt. Servants skin the trophies and prepare the carcasses for cooking.

Days of imperial hunting were typically followed by nights of feasting and merrymaking. On this hunt, Akbar is accompanied by many of his queens. A luxurious harem tent has been set up for them in the centre of the corral.

What feelings does this painting evoke in you? Do you find yourself making a judgement about Mughal character?

A Painter's Life

Artists at Work

Imperial artists worked in large, airy *kitab-khana*s (literally, book houses) like this one. Thick walls kept the interiors cool through the searing Indian summers. Rooms opened on to gardens with verdant lawns, fragrant flowers and bubbling streams.

49

In this *kitab-khana*, Akbar's artists sit in groups on carpeted floors, wooden easels balanced on their knees. A scribe takes dictation. He is surrounded by the tools of his trade—clamshells to hold pigments, bowls of water and ink, and engraved boxes to hold his brushes and pens.

On the verandah, a painter and a calligrapher enjoy some gossip as they work. A little distance away, a young artist smiles at his sketch of a horse rearing up powerfully on its hind legs. Out in the garden, surrounded by watchmen and attendants, a burly papermaker burnishes a sheet of paper, smoothing down its surface in preparation for painting.

Akbar's artists often worked collectively on a painting, each one focusing on what he did best. Some were expert portrait painters, others excelled in animals, yet others painted the backgrounds. Young apprentices started by preparing pigments, binding paintbrushes and burnishing paper until it shone. Then they slowly worked their way up the hierarchy until they finally could paint independently and present their paintings to the king.

***Daulat the Painter and
Abd al-Rahim the Scribe***

Emperor Jehangir, always proud of his artists' skills, commissioned Daulat, the painter, to make a self-portrait. So Daulat cleverly portrayed himself, with easel and paintbrush, at work on a likeness of Abd al-Rahim, the calligrapher seated across from him in this painting.

فلک رایجشت کراینده دار   برو داد و دین هر دو پاینده دار   اتمام یافت وانجام پذیرفت این کتاب گرامی بسم خراست
و کتابخانه عالی سب کان حضرت خلافت پناهی ظل اللهی خسرو جهرمان فاتح چراغ جهان افروز نه طاق ثابت نوای تخت
و هم فرمان فرمای هفت اقلیم شهسوار سعادت رخش ملک ستان بخش جهان بخش قدر شناس کهف هنرمندان منعت بخش یاقوت
بخشندۀ دریای موج حسنی و سپهر ممکلت جود و جهان فوج و درفعت رای و اورنگ پهلوانی   ابو الفتح جلال الدین محمد اکبر

پادشاه غازی خلد الله طلال سلطنه و اقابله کجک رایت سلک نبع قدیم فقیر الحقیر عبد الرحیم درمیست و چهارم ماه از در سال حکم الهی جلوس پیمون پادشاهی امیدیک بصفحه کاینات تمام ونشان قلم و رقم باشد نشو سلطنت و اقبال بطوای عدای آنخضرت سر بلندی امیدی عبرت پای کان یک نهان تمت

همه میدید..

Can you feel the silence and concentration conveyed in this miniature?

The softness of Daulat's gaze, the half-smile playing on the calligrapher's lips, and the easy sitting posture of both men clearly demonstrate the pleasure they take in their work.

Notice the luxuriant carpets as well, the shades rolled up to let the breezes flow, and the niches in the wall, holding beautiful bottles and amphoras.

In the foreground, Daulat has showcased the thoughtfulness of a servant who has placed a little pitcher of cool water to quench the artists' thirst.

Mughal emperors often asked artists to paint portraits of themselves (the artists) or to include themselves in court scenes. Because the emperors took so much interest in their artists' work, the artists enjoyed a special closeness with the emperors. Although they rarely became rich, they could look forward to a comfortable life as long as their work pleased their royal patrons.

Resources

To View Mughal Paintings…

You may view Mughal miniatures at many museums all over the world. Here are a few of them:

NOTE: Most museums do not always have their Mughal miniatures on display for the public. Therefore, please call ahead or check the museum's website for current exhibitions before you visit.

In India:

Prince of Wales Museum, Mumbai: http://www.bombaymuseum.org
National Museum, Delhi: http://www.nationalmuseumindia.gov.in
Indian Museum, Kolkata: http://www.indianmuseumkolkata.org

In the United States:

The Freer Gallery of Art and the Arthur M. Sackler Gallery, Smithsonian Institution, Washington, D.C.: http://www.asia.si.edu
Los Angeles County Museum of Art, Los Angeles: http://www.lacma.org
Fogg Museum of Art, Cambridge: http://www.artmuseums.harvard.edu/fogg

In the United Kingdom:

British Museum, London: http://www.thebritishmuseum.ac.uk
Victoria & Albert Museum, London: http://www.vam.ac.uk
Chester Beatty Library, Dublin: http://www.cbl.ie
This is one of the few museums that has outstanding Mughal miniatures among its permanent displays.

In Europe:

Museum Rietberg, Zurich: http://tinyurl.com/2hr3rw
Musee Guimet, Paris: http://www.museeguimet.fr/-English-

Bibliography

Beach, Milo Cleveland *et al. The King of the World: The Padshahnama: An Imperial Mughal Manuscript from the Royal Library, Windsor Castle.* London: Thames and Hudson, 1997.

Okada, Amina. *Indian Miniatures of the Mughal Court.* Translated by Deke Dusinberre. New York: Harry N. Abrams, 1992.

Pal, Pratapaditya. *Master Artists of the Imperial Mughal Court.* Bombay: Marg Publications, 1991.

Sen, Geeti. *Paintings from the Akbarnama: A Visual Chronicle of Mughal India.* Varanasi: Lustre Press under arrangement with Rupa Publications, 1984.

Welch, Stuart Cary. *Imperial Mughal Painting.* New York: George Braziller, 1978.

———. *India: Art and Culture 1300–1900.* New York: Metropolitan Museum of Art, 1985.